Contents

Introduction

This booklet has been designed to give practical help to family members or friends who have the responsibility of planning the funeral of a loved one.

For some, this will be the first time you have had to perform such a duty. This booklet tries to answer all the questions you are likely to ask. If you follow this booklet's step-by-step approach much of the potential anxiety surrounding the occasion will be allayed.

For others, you will be familiar with much of what is written here, but it will provide a useful checklist as you try to remember all that needs to be done.

A prayer when someone has died

Lord Jesus, I entrust N... into your loving hands. I give you thanks for all the blessings of his/her life, and for the love and friendship we shared together. Send your Holy Spirit at this moment to deepen my faith in your presence and fill me with hope that your promises may be fulfilled for N...: the joy of resurrection and a place in your Father's house. Amen.

Your Feelings

This booklet will be used by a whole host of people, experiencing a great range of emotions. Clearly the grown-up son or daughter of an elderly parent, who has died peacefully after a long and fulfilled life, will be feeling very different from the parent of a young child who has died in a tragic accident. But whatever the circumstances surrounding the death of your loved one, you will be grieving and it is important that you allow yourself and other family members and friends to grieve and give expression to their grief. For many this process is worked through with the support and comfort of one another in the ordinary way, but it is not unusual for people to need specialised support at a time like this.

Even when the death was not unexpected we can sometimes go into a state of shock and disbelief afterwards. Our emotions can be very unpredictable, our mood swings dramatic, and people sometimes feel they just cannot cope. Don't be surprised or embarrassed if you feel you need to consult your doctor or one of the agencies which offer bereavement counselling. A list of such agencies and how they may be contacted is provided in an appendix at the end of this booklet.

It might also be good to remember that sometimes we all find it difficult to know what to say to others when we learn that someone has died in their family, especially when it is unexpected. So, don't be surprised if some of your friends and neighbours fail to respond to you as affectionately and generously as you might hope. It may just be that they do not know what to say or how to respond. You may be able to help them by broaching the subject first. And remember there are those people who, because they find it difficult to express themselves verbally, may just give you a big hug as a sign of their desire to share your sorrow at this difficult time.

A Word of Reassurance

Whether you acquired this booklet yourself or received it from your priest/deacon or funeral director, you are clearly concerned to ensure that you remember everything. People commonly say after a funeral: "That was exactly as he/she would have wanted it", and you may well be hoping that family and friends will say something similar on this occasion. Please remember that you can be confident that all the professionals with whom you will be dealing in preparation for the funeral will want to help in every way.

The Christian Response

Christians often consider that in the face of death they should have greater fai[th] and not be racked with doubts, anxieties and questions. We are all very differer[t]. Sometimes the death of a loved one can bring great consolation and peace, b[ut] at other times we can be surprised at how traumatised we are by the who[le] experience. It is important to know that such feelings are normal and just to be ab[le] to talk them through with someone else can bring comfort and encouragemer[t]. A number of parishes have formed bereavement groups to minister to those wh[o] have lost relatives and friends, and in some instances this is a joint venture wi[th] the other Christian churches in the area. You might like to check whether such [a] group exists where you live if you think it could be helpful.

Such a ministry is very much part of the Christian tradition. Writing to the Thessalonians, Paul told them "to encourage one another", reminding them that their faith in Jesus would fill them with hope in the resurrection and an eternity at peace with God.

Perhaps the most consoling aspect of all this is that our faith is not in a God who is far away in the clouds, but in a God who loved us so much that in Jesus he came among us and shared our experience of life and death. Jesus was saddened when his great friend, Lazarus, died, and he wept. He was deeply distressed at the prospect of his own suffering and death and pleaded with his heavenly Father to take the chalice of his suffering away from him if it were possible.

In the end Jesus was crucified and he handed his life over, praying for forgiveness for those who were responsible. Yet, in spite of his promises to the disciples that he would not leave them orphans, that the Spirit would stay with them and lead them to understand the truth, at first they failed to understand. They were not ready for the resurrection and only gradually put the jigsaw together and saw the picture more clearly.

If the picture is not clear for you at the moment, do n[ot] be surprised. Like the father of the sick boy in Mar[k's] Gospel, we often have to say: "I believe; help n[y] unbelief." For now, just think about these words of Jesu[s]. Do not let your hearts be troubled. Believe in God, [ ] believe also in me. In my Father's house there are [ ] many dwelling places. If it were not so, would I hav[e] told you that I go to prepare a place for you? And i[f] go and prepare a place for you, I will come again a[nd] will take you to myself, so that where I am, there yo[u] may be also.

Christian funerals return over and over again to t[he] theme of Christ rising from the dead because th[is] mystery is at the very heart of our faith. It is so import[ant] that St Paul said: "If Christ has not been raised, your fa[ith] is futile and you are still in your sins." Of course t[he] service will be a personal one for you and your fam[ily] appropriate to the one who has died. At the same ti[me] every Christian funeral is centred throughout on t[he] source of our hope, Jesus, who came that we might [be] raised with him to the glory of heaven.

"I believe; help my unbelief."

who to contact / what to do

Three key people will help you with all the arrangements and will interact with you and each other:
the **Doctor**, the **Funeral Director** and the **Priest.**

The **Doctor** (and in certain situations: the coroner, the police)

When someone dies, it is the legal requirement to have the death certified by a qualified doctor. This will be straightforward if the death occurred in hospital or the deceased has been attended to by the GP through a terminal illness. If the death was in any way sudden or unexpected, then the doctor will have to refer the matter to the coroner and the body may need to be examined to determine the cause of death. Generally this is a straightforward process and should not be a cause for concern, nor should it delay the making of the funeral arrangements. It is a safeguard for everyone and a reminder

of how protective society is of our welfare. If someone h been found dead unexpectedly it is important to inform t police and they will determine if there are any suspicic circumstances which should be investigated. Only situations where a crime has been committed, the dea was as the result of an accident or there is concern abc whether all the appropriate medical procedures we followed, is it likely that there will have to be an inquest. such circumstances the release of the body and theref the funeral may have to be delayed.

The **Funeral Director** (Undertaker)

Remember that you are free to select the funeral director of your choice and may wish to ask trusted friends or acquaintances for their recommendations. It is advisable to choose a funeral director who is a member of a recognised trade association (e.g. The National Association of Funeral Directors or The Society of Allied and Independent Funeral Directors). Then you can be sure they will abide by a strict code of practice. Also you may choose to ask

for quotations from more than one funeral director to compare prices and the services they offer. The priest or deacon at the church may be able to advise and will know the funeral directors in the district, particularly those that are understanding and co-operative when it comes to Christian funerals. By the same token the funeral directors will know the clergy, and should you not be familiar with the local scene, they will be able to introduce you to them.

Suffice it to say that, generally, funeral directors are very aware of the stresses and strains you will be facing. They will know the procedures that will be necessary and will guide you gently through all that is required. They will be experienced in dealing with the medical services, the coroner's court and the civi authorities, so, should you encounter any difficulties, do not hesitate to check with them.

The **Priest** (The Church's Minister)

Please note that the ordinary minister for a funeral is the priest or deacon. Of course, if you have a service of Holy Communion, the priest will preside.

It may be that the priest, deacon or minister has been attending the deceased person before they died, in which case the planning for the funeral will be part of a continuing

ministry to the deceased person and to you and the fam If you have not been in touch with the clergy, then it will important to contact them as soon as possible so that th and the funeral director can liaise with you over times a venues.

Registering the death

For the funeral directors and clergy to be able to proceed with the burial or cremation, it would normally be necessary for the death to be registered at the registrar's office which covers the sub-district in which the death occurred. It is possible to supply the relevant information to any registrar in England and Wales. However, if you attend a register office other than the one for the sub-district where the death occurred, the certificates will need to be forwarded in the post, thereby possibly causing a delay.

If you do not know the location of the register office, the funeral director will be able to advise you, along with its opening times and whether you are required to make an appointment. It is as well to check these matters before going so as not to experience any unnecessary frustration.

Below are some official notes to guide the person who takes on the task of registering the death

The Medical Certificate of Death may be available at the doctor's surgery, hospital or nursing home, depending on the circumstances. You will need to take this to the registrar together with the deceased's **Medical Card** (if available).

Duties of informant

When the death is registered the informant must be prepared to give to the registrar the following particulars relating to the deceased:

1. The date and place of death.
2. The full name and surname (and maiden surname if the deceased was a woman who had married).
3. The date and place of birth.
4. The occupation (and if the deceased was a married woman or a widow the name and occupation of her husband).
5. The usual address.
6. Whether the deceased was in receipt of a pension or allowance from public funds.
7. If the deceased was married, the date of birth of the surviving widow or widower.

Persons qualified and liable to act as informants

The following persons are designated by the Births and Deaths Registration Act 1953 as qualified to give information concerning a death; in order of preference they are:

Deaths in houses and public institutions

1. A relative of the deceased, present at the death.
2. A relative of the deceased, in attendance during the last illness.
3. A relative of the deceased, residing or being in the sub-district where the death occurred.
4. A person present at the death.
5. The occupier* if he/she knew of the happening of the death.
6. Any inmate if he/she knew of the happening of the death.
7. The person causing the disposal of the body.

Deaths not in houses or dead bodies found

1. Any relative of the deceased having knowledge of any of the particulars required to be registered.
2. Any person present at the death.
3. Any person who found the body.
4. Any person in charge of the body.
5. The person causing the disposal of the body.

Involvement of the coroner

One further piece of information concerns the situation when the matter is referred to the coroner. As with the doctor's certificate, the registrar will not be able to proceed without document certifying the cause of death from the coroner. Therefore be careful to ensure that you have this document or that it has been delivered directly to the registrar's office by the coroner.

PLEASE NOTE: Once the registrar has issued a Green Certificate (for burial or cremation) you must hand this to your chosen funeral director as soon as possible. Without it the funeral cannot take place.

Finally it is worth noting that when registering the death it is helpful if you know how many copies of the death certificate you will require, not least because such copies are cheaper then than if you return later for more. Banks, building societies and other official bodies will require officially certified copies when matters concerning the estate of the deceased person have to be sorted out. However, all these organisations are very good at returning the said document as soon as they have seen it and verified the death, so you may not feel you need one for every organisation to be contacted.

Removal of the body

In the case of an expected death at a private address or nursing home, the funeral director can remove the deceased once the attending doctor has agreed to issue a death certificate. However, this may not be the case if death occurs in hospital, as most hospitals now require a copy of the registrar's Green Certificate before removal can take place. Local custom or family preferences may determine that the remains are laid out for a period before removal from the home or hospital. Sometimes people wish to have the deceased returned to their home or laid in a chapel of rest prior to the funeral. These are all matters which can be discussed with your funeral director.

Viewing the body

Again local custom and family preferences will differ, but all funeral directors are very accommodating should family members and friends wish to view and pray beside the body of the deceased in the days prior to the funeral. The funeral director's premises will have a quiet room or chapel where this can be done. It is simply a question of making the necessary arrangements regarding dates and times.

---

* "Occupier" in relation to a public institution includes the governor, keeper, master, matron, superintendent, or other chief resident officer.

(Please note that at the time of publication the government has produced a consultative document on the registration of births, marriages and deaths. Therefore the practices above are subject to any change which future legislation may introduce. Cf the General Register Office website www.gro.gov.uk)

Preparing the funeral service
Introduction

Clearly the more involved the family and friends of the deceased person can be in arranging the funeral service the more satisfactory it will usually be. However, by the same token there are many people who ardly know where to begin, and, perhaps verwhelmed by the sadness of the occasion, prefer to ave most of the arrangements to the priest or minister. such is the case you should not feel guilty, but be epared for the clergy to check with you that their uggestions are appropriate.

ome people have thought and prayed about their neral and left detailed instructions. In such rcumstances it is usually just a case of honouring their wishes and being grateful to them for having been so thoughtful. But of course many others have left no instructions, preferring to leave it to the discretion of family and friends to decide what is appropriate.

Where family and friends are able to work together to prepare the service, this can be very beneficial and therapeutic for all concerned. It enables those who are mourning to put their energy into something practical and directly related to their loved one. This can contribute greatly to the healing part of the bereavement process. Indeed such interaction with others is a good example of that quiet ministry of care and mutual support, which enables us to fulfil St Paul's advice to "encourage one another".

BEFORE
the FUNERAL

Prior to the reception of the body into the church, it is customary in some places to arrange a prayer vigil either at home or at the funeral director's chapel. Indeed sometimes such a vigil may take place in the church, if the body is received the evening before the funeral service.

Reception into the church

In some places the tradition of receiving the body into the church on the evening before the funeral is still the norm. This is always accompanied by a short service and for a special reason may include the celebration of Holy Communion, also called the Eucharist. Then the body remains peacefully in the church overnight until the funeral the following day. However, it should be noted that this custom is not encouraged everywhere. The local clergy will be able to advise you on this as on all matters relating to church services.

Many people will wish to have the funeral service in the parish church and then proceed to the cemetery or the crematorium. If the body has not been received the evening before it will be received into the church immediately before the funeral service. In other cases the choice may be simply to go straight to the chapel in the cemetery or crematorium.

The Church has set forms for all these services with a variety of options in

terms of readings and prayers. They all conclude with the prayers of committal either at the graveside or in preparation for the cremation.

In discussing the options with the clergy and the funeral director it will be important to clarify what you require and determine the approximate timings. Here the clergy and the funeral director will be able to advise. They will understand the logistics, including allowing time to cope with the traffic between the two sites.

FUNERAL
SERVICE

For churchgoers, a service of Holy Communion may be part of the funeral

service. If this takes place more tir will probably be required for the chur service than in other traditior especially if a large congregation expected and many people are likely be receiving Holy Communion.*

However, for those who do not go church very often there is the option having a funeral service without t celebration of the Eucharist. This avoi the embarrassment that can arise ov the reception of Holy Communion.

It is also possible to have the fune service at the crematorium or t cemetery chapel. Whatever kind service you choose, you can be sure will be according to the rites of t Church and conducted with the dign due to those who have died.

---

* In the Anglican Church, anyone who is used to receiving Holy Communion in their own church is welcome to share the bread and wine. But this can still be awkward for people who do not regularly go to church. If you think that there will be quite a few people in the congregation in that position, the priest will be happy to give them directions about receiving Holy Communion. The death of a family member or close friend may be an occasion to reflect again on our lives and renew our commitment to the Lord, so this may be a specially appropriate time to share in Holy Communion.

Scripture Readings

We have already noted the emphasis on the resurrection in Christian funerals and how this is coupled with the understanding that Jesus shared in the pain and suffering of the world and the sadness of death. On this occasion it is recommended that the readings from Scripture should reflect these elements: our faith in and hope for the resurrection, as well as our own experience of pain and loss.

In the lectionary a large number of readings has been selected from both the Old and New Testaments to help us focus on these mysteries. In a separate insert with this booklet we list the references to all these readings and include the full texts of some of the most commonly used. However, it should also be noted that you are not limited to these texts, should the deceased person have expressed some particular preference or you regard another Scripture text as especially appropriate.

It is usual to choose two or three readings and a psalm: one from the Old Testament, and/or one from the New Testament letters and usually one from the Gospels.

Other Readings

It is becoming more common for people to choose other readings as well as Scripture readings and the following guidelines may be helpful. There will be different customs locally and it will be important to talk this through with the clergy beforehand. A poem or piece of writing other than the Scriptures may be particularly appropriate in helping the congregation to meditate on the deceased person's life and work, especially if it is one of their favourite pieces or even a composition of their own.

In a celebration of the Eucharist, however, it is good to remember that, as at all such celebrations, the Liturgy of the Word is specifically focused on the Scriptures. Therefore another reading of this kind would probably fit more easily as a meditation after Holy Communion or as part of the committal ceremony.

Sermons, Homilies and Addresses

It is usual for the clergy to give a sermon or homily after the readings. The purpose of this is to help the congregation focus on the promises of Jesus and our hopes for the one who has died. It is also an opportunity to remember them with affection and love. If the person was well known to the priest, the homily will undoubtedly include a reflection in thanksgiving for their life and stories illustrating the Christian context of their life.

In the situation where the clergy are not familiar with the deceased, it is becoming common for a member of the family or a close friend to say a few words about the person.

Again it is important to note that such an address should not replace the homily, so is more fitting at the end before the coffin is removed from the church.

Also it should be noted that if there is no one who would feel confident to say a few words or give an address, the clergy would be only too willing to listen to your memories and incorporate them into what they will say during the homily.

The Prayers of Intercession

There are some sample prayers of intercession in the separate booklet of readings, but clearly if you are able to prepare your own, this is a wonderful opportunity to give expression to your concerns and feelings before God. As a general principle, these prayers should be short and to the point. They are offered to God the Father through Jesus Christ. They should introduce the focus of the prayer (e.g. for the deceased person and what we hope for them; for all present and ourselves; for the wider needs of the Church and the community).

Offertory Procession

In some places the family of the deceased bring up the gifts of bread and wine to be used at the funeral Eucharist. These gifts are symbols of ourselves and our offering to God. They express our desire to be united with Christ and one day with our loved one in heaven.

Music

Music is an integral part of the Church's liturgy. Much will depend here on local custom and the availability of musicians and singers. The clergy will be able to advise on what is possible and will usually be very happy to accommodate if there is musical talent in the family or you have a friend who plays the organ. It is really important to talk this through well beforehand to avoid disappointment or misunderstanding. Today there is a rich variety of music, both traditional and modern. At the same time tastes can differ greatly, and especially when it comes to the playing of pre-recorded music, there can sometimes be disagreements about what is acceptable in church. Where such disagreements occur, it may be worth considering whether another form of commemoration in another setting and at another time might not be more suitable to recall memories of favourite musical pieces, as also the prose and poetry mentioned above.

To assist you in coming to decisions over music, Appendix One includes some suggestions, and the priest who conducts the funeral will also be able to advise you.

BURIAL OR CREMATION

An important decision that has to be taken is whether the body will be buried or cremated. This may not be a difficult decision because often our friends and relatives have expressed a clear preference during their lifetime and usually we would honour the wishes in this matter. However, if the is uncertainty or doubt, it is importa to consult with the rest of the fam and try to reach agreement so that th does not become a source of confli or unhappiness.

Some Christians may be concerne about cremation because ur relatively recently cremation wa unusual in the Church. It is importa to know that this is no longer the cas The old feeling about cremation has be understood in its historical conte when cremation was used as a argument against the resurrection the body. It was never a matter doctrine and today Christians shou be totally at peace should they choo cremation. We believe that the Lo raised us from the dust of the ear and will refashion the dust of o mortal bodies into his own likenes (See Philippians 3:21.)

It is also worth noting that there is no a special service for the Burial Ashes. Generally this is easy organise after the day of the funeral, a date and place for the convenien of all concerned.

Burial at Sea

In situations where the deceas person was a seafarer, there a special prayers in the rite for burial sea.

Selected Glossary

Obsequies: Funeral rites.

Prayer of Commendation: This prayer is a commendation of the deceased person to God and is said before the coffin leaves the church or in a service at the cemetery or crematorium chapel before the actual burial or cremation.

Prayer of Committal: This is the prayer which is said immediately before the burial the cremation.

Symbols

Symbols help us to focus our thoughts and feelings. Certain Christian symbols have regularly been used at funerals over the years, and the Church encourages you to think about which ones you would like at the funeral of your friend or relative. Here we describe a number of symbols for you. You will be able to discuss with your minister which of these would be most appropriate in your church and for your family.

Flowers

Wreaths, sprays and bouquets are common at most funerals, but again customs and expectations may vary. Sometimes it is the expressed wish of the family that donations be given to a particular charity in lieu of flowers. Perhaps the only flowers would be those of the immediate family. Whatever decisions are made it is important to try and ensure that all the key members of the family are in agreement. Then whatever is decided should be conveyed to all other family members and friends to avoid upset or confusion on the day.

Again customs differ and the clergy and funeral director will advise on what is usual in the local church. The funeral director will always look after the flowers and ensure that they can be viewed by the mourners, following either the service at the crematorium or the committal at the graveside, where they will often be placed on the grave once it has been filled in. Sometimes other arrangements for the use of the flowers may be made by the family.

Your funeral director or the clergy will be pleased to advise what is feasible or usual in your parish.

The Paschal Candle

Always at the head of the coffin stands the Paschal (Easter) Candle, a symbol of the Risen Christ, the Light of the World. It is from this candle that at Baptism a small candle representing the person being baptised is lit and we are reminded that Jesus told us to be the light of the world. For the deceased person things have now come full circle.

Incense

Another sign of reverence is the use of incense, which may be used in the usual way during the celebration of Communion and also during the prayers of commendation, prior to leaving the church. It reminds us that our prayers on behalf of our loved one rise up with Jesus to our Father in heaven.

The Cross

We are marked by the sign of the cro at our baptism because Jes commanded us to take up our cro and follow him. Because it w through the cross that Jesus came the resurrection, it is wholly fitting th a cross or crucifix should be placed the coffin or previously fixed as attachment to the coffin.

Holy Water

Holy water is used on a number occasions, and it is always a reminder our baptism whereby we first becor members of Christ's Church a therefore heirs to his kingdom. The co may be sprinkled with holy water when is received into the church and at t end of the funeral, before it is carried o At the graveside the grave itself may blessed with holy water and a prayer consecrate the ground offere reminding us of Jesus' own burial. T custom often proves very consoling young and old alike. (In some places i also the custom to sprinkle some ea at the same time, reminding us that return to the dust from which we cam

The Pall

Although a custom not yet wid used, the placing over the coffin o white cloth, called a pall, is anoth option for those who wish to str their faith in the resurrection. The pa another symbol of our baptism and reminder of the white shawl plac around us on that occasion. T whiteness speaks to us of Chris death and resurrection by which will be made spotless and prepared the kingdom of heaven.

The Book of the Gospels

The book of the Gospels may placed on the coffin and this accompanied by a prayer. Clearly if deceased person had a perso Bible it would be fitting to use t (At a priest's funeral the stole – sym of his or her priestly ministry – is a placed on the coffin.)

The death of a child

There can be nothing more distressing than for parents to have to bury their own child. Whether the child lived for some years, died soon after birth, or was stillborn, the sorrow may be almost unbearable. Parents, family and the Christian community are faced with bewildering and hard questions at such a time, and should not feel guilty about their anger and pain. One of the prayers that you might find helpful at this time is: "O God, who brought us to birth, and in whose arms we die, in our grief and shock, contain and comfort us; embrace us with your love, give us hope in our confusion and grace to let go into new life; through Jesus Christ. Amen."

Special Rites

There is a variety of special prayers and services available for the funerals of babies and children. The clergy and the funeral directors will be especially sensitive and thoughtful in ensuring that you are able to select what is appropriate for you and your child.

Miscarriage

Miscarriage can bring as much sadness as the death of a child after it has been born. Miscarriage is defined in law as when a child is stillborn prior to 24 weeks of pregnancy. It can prove traumatically painful for the parents and especially the mother. At one time families were left to cope with the aftermath of a miscarriage by themselves. Today, with the realisation of the sacredness of the unborn child, there is more help available and again we refer you to our list of agencies at the end of the booklet. The child/foetus is still termed as human remains and therefore a funeral can be arranged, though this would be unusual. On the other hand it may be helpful to arrange a short memorial service, thereby placing this unborn baby into the hands of God. Special prayers are provided in the prayer book to be used at the funeral or memorial service after a miscarriage or a still birth.

Remember that professional help is available and we include addresses and contact numbers at the end of this booklet.

Questions people ask

What will the funeral cost?

Some people will have made provision for their funeral with life insurance or similar policies, but, as with everything, the cost of a funeral may pose real anxieties for those responsible for it. The funeral director will always discuss the costs with you from the outset and much will depend on what type of coffin you choose and how many cars you wish to accompany the hearse. There is usually a standard fee for the crematorium, clergy and other services like organists, which your funeral director looks after and pays to the respective parties on your behalf. If burial is required, it should be remembered that grave charges can vary greatly between cemeteries. Your funeral director will advise. If you have financial difficulties, do not be afraid to discuss these with those concerned and remember there is no harm in seeking quotations and comparing costs. Help may be available in certain circumstances from the Department of Work and Pensions (formerly the DSS) and your funeral director will be able to advise as to whether you are likely to be eligible for such assistance. Certainly when it comes to the Church, if you are in serious financial difficulty the clergy may well be willing to waive any fee. It is not usual for the Church to charge a fee for a baby under one year old.

Your minister or priest will be able to show you the table of fees for funerals in the Church of England, or you can look it up for yourself, if you have access to the internet, on www.cofe.anglican.org/lifeevents.

There is to be an autopsy on my father's body and I am worried whether this means that body parts will be removed.
Because of the publicity over the removal of body parts at the time of some post-mortem examinations and the distress this has caused, there is a far greater sensitivity over these matters today. It is important that you ask all the questions you wish of the coroner so that your mind is at peace when your father is buried.

The death in our family was the result of suicide. Is it possible to have a Christian funeral in such circumstances?
It is true that in the past there were difficulties over Christian burial following suicide. Today no such problem exists. Indeed the Church now makes special provision among the prayers for such an occasion. Rightly the presumption is that the person had reached such a distressed state that they were not responsible for their actions. The matter is left calmly and confidently in the hands of God, and the Church will also take great care to minister to the family and friends, who may be particularly traumatised because of the circumstances.
(Please note in Appendix Two an agency that can be contacted by relatives and friends after suicide.)

What should happen to my wife's ashes after the cremation?
There is a special service for the burial of the ashes. This usually happens soon after the funeral. The ashes can be buried in a churchyard, or in the Garden of Remembrance at the crematorium. Your priest or funeral director will be able to advise you.

I want the priest to wear white vestments for my Mum's funeral, but my sister wants purple. Who is right?
Once again we are not in the realms of right and wrong. The purple vestments put the emphasis on our share in the passion and death of Jesus, our need for forgiveness, and the waiting and penance associated with Advent and Lent. The white vestments put the emphasis on the resurrection and the fact that Jesus promised he was going to prepare a place for us in his Father's house. Again you will need to talk this through within the family and with the priest who will probably have vestments that he or she usually wears at a funeral.

Our family is not really a practising one. Should we settle for a funeral service or have a Holy Communion service as well?
This is a difficult question and much depends on what in the end you will be comfortable with and consider right for your family and your deceased relative. Clearly this may be an opportunity for you to reflect on how you see the future. Hopefully the loving support of the church community will be bringing you great comfort and helping you realise that we are all precious in the eyes of God. Talk it over with the minister or other members of the church community. If it is not appropriate to have Holy Communion at the funeral, you can always come to Holy Communion another time, and ask the minister to remember your deceased relative and your family in the prayers at the service.

Can Christians be cremated? The simple answer is "yes". Please see p.14.

Should I take my young child to the funeral?
This is one of those questions to which there is no simple answer. Parents should be able to judge what is best from their knowledge of their children and after discussing it with them. Explain what is going to happen and that people may be upset. Generally children are more resilient than we imagine. They will have to face the reality of death in their lives and this may be a real opportunity to deepen their understanding and their faith.

Our child was stillborn and therefore not baptised. Does this mean that she cannot go to heaven?
Today the prayers of the Church in such situations make it abundantly clear that the Lord's saving presence can reach beyond the physical celebration of the sacrament, redeem this child with the grace of baptism and take her to heaven.

My sister did not attend church after she divorced and remarried in a register office. Will we be able to have a Christian funeral for her?
At the heart of the Gospel is Jesus' compassionate teaching: "Judge not and you will not be judged." However close we are to someone, we never truly know what is going on in their lives or the state of their relationship with God. Like everyone else, in death your sister is entitled to all the funeral rites of the Church.

Should all the family travel in cars provided by the undertaker?
There are no set rules about this. Often close members of the family wish to save themselves any anxiety on the day and arrange to be transported, but equally family and friends are often willing to help out and save costs. As far as possible it is important to let everyone know what is happening and to give the undertaker a good idea of how many private cars will be in the cortège.

My husband was not a Christian but was truly supportive of the children and me and on special occasions came to church with us. Is it possible for him to have a service or even a Eucharist and be buried from the church?
It would be wholly appropriate in such a situation for your husband to be buried from the church and for you and your friends and family to share in the Eucharist at the funeral service.

After the funeral

After the funeral there will probably remain a lot of practical issues to be dealt with. We offer a few hints on how to approach these questions.

A reception for the mourners

Many families organise a social gathering after the funeral service either at home, in a parish centre or at a hotel. Again local custom, personal preferences and finance will determine the arrangements. Such gatherings provide an opportunity for the family to thank those who have come to the funeral and to share memories with them. With all the other preparations that have to be made it is important to ensure that one or two individuals do not carry the load of all the practical and administrative work. Delegating responsibilities in matters such as this is essential.

It is worth noting that some families consider the reception to be the appropriate setting for giving personal addresses about the deceased person as well as playing pieces of their favourite music.

Wills

If the deceased person has left a will and clear directions as to who is to be the executor, then it should be relatively easy to have the will certified and proceed with disposing of the estate. If not, it may be wise to seek legal advice as to how to proceed.

If there are not large sums of money or expensive property to be disposed of, you may find that most of those with whom you have to deal (e.g. banks, building societies and insurance companies) will be satisfied with a copy of the will, signed by a Commissioner for Oaths. Failing that, you will probably need to apply for probate (the process which establishes the validity of the will) or, if there is no will, determine who is entitled to act as administrator of the deceased person's estate (Letters of Administration). In such circumstances it is advisable to seek the assistance of a solicitor or specialist probate company.

Wills can give rise to tensions within families. Try to be sensitive and keep all interested parties informed at each stage to avoid unnecessary upset.

Memorial Stone

If your deceased relative or friend has been buried, you will probably wish to arrange a memorial stone to mark the grave. Also crematoriums often make provision for you to have various types of memorials within the crematorium grounds. Again the funeral director will be able to give you all the necessary information and advice on the cost of the different options.

Checklist

- [ ] Doctor's certificate

- [ ] Contact a funeral director

- [ ] Contact the priest

- [ ] Register the death at the register office

- [ ] Obtain the number of death certificates you think you will need

- [ ] Give the certificate for disposal (Green Certificate) to the funeral director

- [ ] Check any explicit funeral wishes of the deceased person

- [ ] Arrange the details of the ceremonies with the priest and/or deacon

- [ ] Ensure that all who should be informed are informed of the death

- [ ] Make decisions about flowers, donations etc., and inform all concerned

- [ ] Determine how many cars you wish to hire to accompany the hearse

- [ ] Contact all those who will be taking part: readers, musicians etc.

- [ ] Organise the reception (if there is to be one)

- [ ] Ensure that payments are made (usually through the funeral director)

- [ ] After the funeral, deal with the estate of the deceased person

- [ ] Have the will certified and arrange probate if necessary

- [ ] Settle with everyone who is included in the will

- [ ] If appropriate, arrange for a memorial stone

Some music suggestions

Your minister will suggest some points where hymns can be sung, but you can ask for a hymn to come at any suitable point in the service.

Traditional Hymns
Abide with me
All my hope on God is founded
Be thou my vision
Firmly I believe and truly
For all the saints
Guide me, O thou great Redeemer
I heard the voice of Jesus say
Jesus lives, thy terrors now
Jesus, lover of my soul
Jesus, Son of Mary
Lead, kindly light
Let Saints on Earth in concert sing
Lord Jesus, think on me
Lord of all hopefulness
Now the green blade riseth
O bread of heaven
O God, our help in ages past
O Jesus, I have promised
Praise to the holiest in the height
Praise we our God with joy
Sing with all the saints in glory
Soul of my Saviour
The lamb's high banquet
The strife is o'er the battle done
Thine be the glory

Modern Hymns and Songs
Abba father, let me be
Be not afraid
Be still and know I am with you
Go, silent friend
How great thou art
I am the bread of life
I, the Lord of sea and sky
I watch the sunrise
Jesu, son of Mary
Like a child that rests
Make me a channel of your peace
O the love of my Lord
On eagle's wings
Such love
There is a longing in our hearts
There is a Redeemer

(You may also find suitable hymns in the following categories in the hymn book used in the parish: Anointing and Healing, Comfort, Eternal Life, Faith, Guidance, Hope and Trust, Love of God for us, Peace, Praise, Funeral, Easter)

Taizé Chants
Bless the Lord, my soul
In the Lord I'll be ever thankful
Jesus, remember me
O Christe, Domine Jesu
O Lord, hear my prayer

Psalms
It is usual to have a psalm in a funeral service, though it may be in a metrical or hymn version, or can be replaced with a scriptural song or canticle.

Psalm 23: The Lord's my shepherd **or** The King of love my shepherd is

Psalm 103: Praise, my soul, the King of heaven

Psalm 42: As longs the deer

Songs of Farewell
May the choirs of angels
Saints of God
I know that my redeemer lives